Project 7-11

Back to Basics

MATHS

for 10-11 year olds

George Rodda

Letts

Addition and subtraction

32 star players have entered this competition.

Fill in this table showing the number of players for each round and the number of matches.

Round	1	2	3	Semi-final	Final
Number of players	32	16			
Number of matches	16			2	1

What was the total number of matches played? ☐

How many matches would be needed altogether

for an entry of 64 players? ☐

Find these totals.

```
 639     499     609     746
+471    +501    +391    +284
____    ____    ____    ____

____    ____    ____    ____
```

Work out these differences.

```
 431     507     600     987
-229    -409    -237    -789
____    ____    ____    ____

____    ____    ____    ____
```

Fill in the total for each of these players.

Player	Alan	Betty	Chris	Don	Edith
Score for round 1	141	302	237	402	363
Score for round 2	52	109	143	299	237
Total					

Fill in the missing score for each player.

Player	Fred	Gill	Heidi	Ian	Jo	Kim
Score	300	299	301	291	259	249
Needed to make 500	200					
Total	500	500	500	500	500	500

Find the total and write down how many more are needed to make 400.

	60	100	120	25
	140	20	120	15
	+ 101	+ 2	+ 5	+ 4
	____	____	____	____
Score needed:	☐	☐	☐	☐

For each of these sums write in two of the numbers **4, 5, 6, 7** to make the sum correct.

7☐	☐6	4☐	7☐
+ ☐4	+ 5☐	+ ☐7	+ ☐4
1 3 0	1 0 3	1 2 2	1 3 9

☐6	7☐	☐5	☐4
− 5☐	− ☐5	− 4☐	− 5☐
2 2	3 1	1 8	1 8

Multiplication

In 3 years this cow should give

$$\begin{array}{r} 1500 \\ \times \quad 3 \\ \hline 4500 \\ \hline \end{array}$$ litres of milk.

At the rate of 1500 litres of milk a year for each cow, fill in this table:

Number of cows	1	2	3	4	5
Number of litres in 1 year	1500				

Now fill in this table using the rate of 1500 litres a year for each cow.

Milk given by	1 cow	2 cows	
in 1 year	1500		litres
in 2 years			litres
in 3 years			litres
in 4 years		12000	litres

Work out these multiplication sums.

$$\begin{array}{r} 1500 \\ \times \quad 5 \\ \hline \\ \hline \end{array} \qquad \begin{array}{r} 1500 \\ \times \quad 6 \\ \hline \\ \hline \end{array} \qquad \begin{array}{r} 1500 \\ \times \quad 7 \\ \hline \\ \hline \end{array} \qquad \begin{array}{r} 1500 \\ \times \quad 8 \\ \hline \\ \hline \end{array}$$

125×3 = $\qquad$ 126×3 = $\qquad$ 123×6 = $\qquad$ 222×5 =

$$\begin{array}{r} 205 \\ \times \quad 9 \\ \hline \\ \hline \end{array} \qquad \begin{array}{r} 178 \\ \times \quad 8 \\ \hline \\ \hline \end{array} \qquad \begin{array}{r} 420 \\ \times \quad 5 \\ \hline \\ \hline \end{array} \qquad \begin{array}{r} 199 \\ \times \quad 9 \\ \hline \\ \hline \end{array}$$

Fill in this multiplication square.

×	1	2	3	4	5	6	7	8	9	10
1										
2			6							
3										
4						24				
5										
6										
7										
8										
9										
10										

The answers in the box belong to the sums below.

860		747
	1836	
2919		1827
	4527	
1476		2160

Put the answers in the right place.

$$\begin{array}{r} 172 \\ \times \quad 5 \\ \hline \\ \hline \end{array} \qquad \begin{array}{r} 270 \\ \times \quad 8 \\ \hline \\ \hline \end{array} \qquad \begin{array}{r} 203 \\ \times \quad 9 \\ \hline \\ \hline \end{array} \qquad \begin{array}{r} 249 \\ \times \quad 3 \\ \hline \\ \hline \end{array}$$

$$\begin{array}{r} 306 \\ \times \quad 6 \\ \hline \\ \hline \end{array} \qquad \begin{array}{r} 492 \\ \times \quad 3 \\ \hline \\ \hline \end{array} \qquad \begin{array}{r} 503 \\ \times \quad 9 \\ \hline \\ \hline \end{array} \qquad \begin{array}{r} 417 \\ \times \quad 7 \\ \hline \\ \hline \end{array}$$

Division

This piggy bank is full of coins.
It has 240 one penny coins in it.

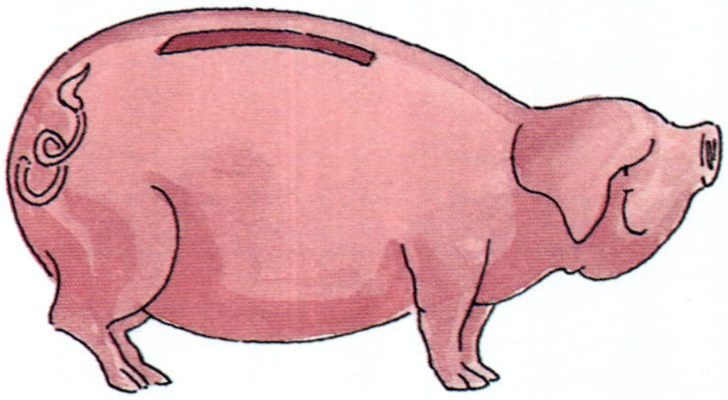

Ian, Emma and Mary share the money.

They have 240p ÷ 3 = 80p each.

From 240p:
how many children could have

10p each?	☐
5p each?	☐
20p each?	☐
40p each?	☐

How many could have 50p ☐ children

and how much would be left? ☐ p

Finish these division sums.

$4\overline{)84}$	$3\overline{)84}$	$6\overline{)84}$	$7\overline{)84}$
$4\overline{)840}$	$5\overline{)840}$	$6\overline{)840}$	$7\overline{)840}$
$2\overline{)840}$	$3\overline{)840}$	$8\overline{)840}$	$10\overline{)840}$
$2\overline{)804}$	$3\overline{)804}$	$6\overline{)804}$	$6\overline{)408}$

Write down the answer and the remainder.

$2\overline{)50}$ rem O

$4\overline{)50}$ rem ______

$6\overline{)50}$ rem ______

$2\overline{)500}$ rem ______

$4\overline{)500}$ rem ______

$6\overline{)500}$ rem ______

$50 \div 10$ = ______ rem ______

$50 \div 8$ = ______ rem ______

$50 \div 3$ = ______ rem ______

$500 \div 10$ = ______ rem ______

$500 \div 8$ = ______ rem ______

$500 \div 3$ = ______ rem ______

The divisors of 14 are 1, 2, 7 and 14.

Fill in the missing divisors.

27 is divisible by 1, 3, ____, 27

25 is divisible by 1, ____, 25

28 is divisible by 1, ____, ____, ____, 14,28

24 is divisible by 1, ____, ____, ____, ____, ____, ____, 24

36 is divisible by 1, ____, ____, ____, ____, ____, ____, ____, 36

29 is divisible by ____, ____

Work out the answers to these divisions.
Some of them have remainders.

$275 \div 5$ = ______

$275 \div 6$ = ______

$275 \div 7$ = ______

$207 \div 4$ = ______

$632 \div 5$ = ______

$900 \div 8$ = ______

$640 \div 6$ = ______

$891 \div 9$ = ______

$1011 \div 10$ = ______

Graphs

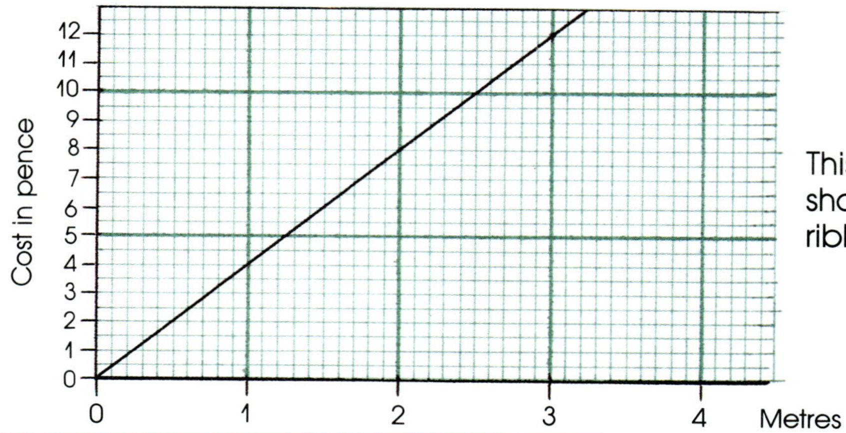

This is part of a graph showing the cost of ribbon at 4p per metre.

At 4p per metre:

2 metres will cost ____ p

3 metres will cost ____ p

2½ metres will cost ____ p

1½ metres will cost ____ p

Use the graph to check your answers.

Mary can peel potatoes at the rate of
20 potatoes in 40 minutes.

At this rate of peeling how long will it take to peel

10 potatoes? ______ minutes

30 potatoes? ______ minutes

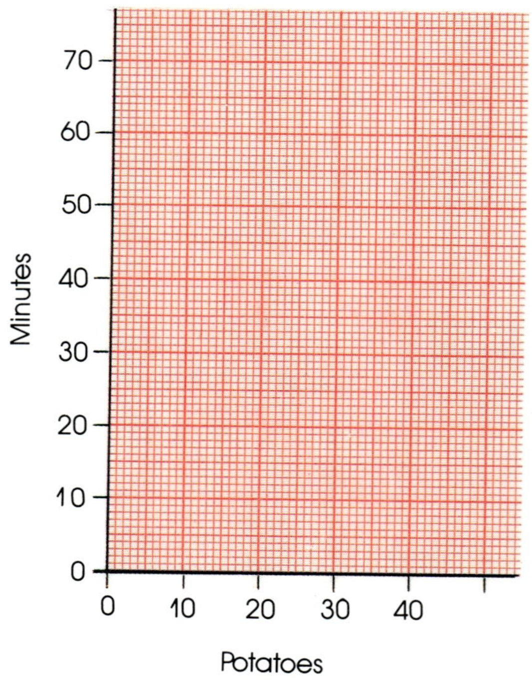

On this graph draw a line showing Mary's time taken to peel potatoes.

What is the average time taken by Mary to peel 1 potato?

______ minutes

This graph shows the results of the bottom team in the league. From the 40 games Atrocious City won ______,

lost ______,

drew ______.

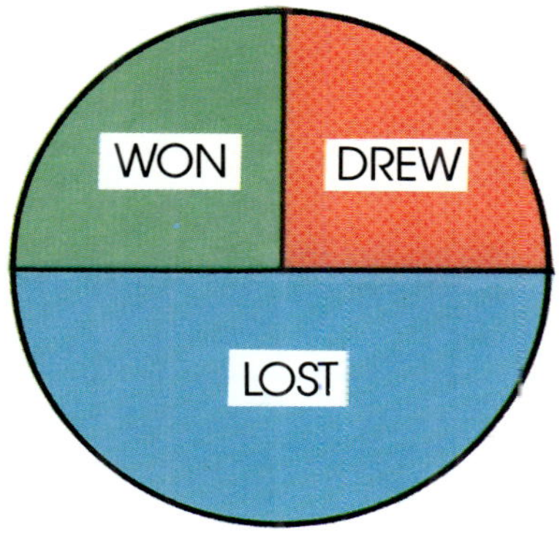

Results for Atrocious City (40 games)

This is the graph for the top team. From the 40 games Wonderhampton won ______,

lost ______,

drew ______.

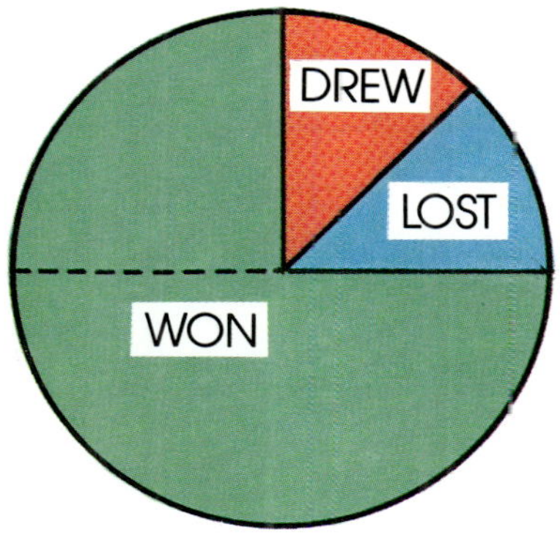

Results for Wonderhampton Rovers (40 games)

This is a graph of Mary's journey which started from her home. She ran, rested for a while and then walked.

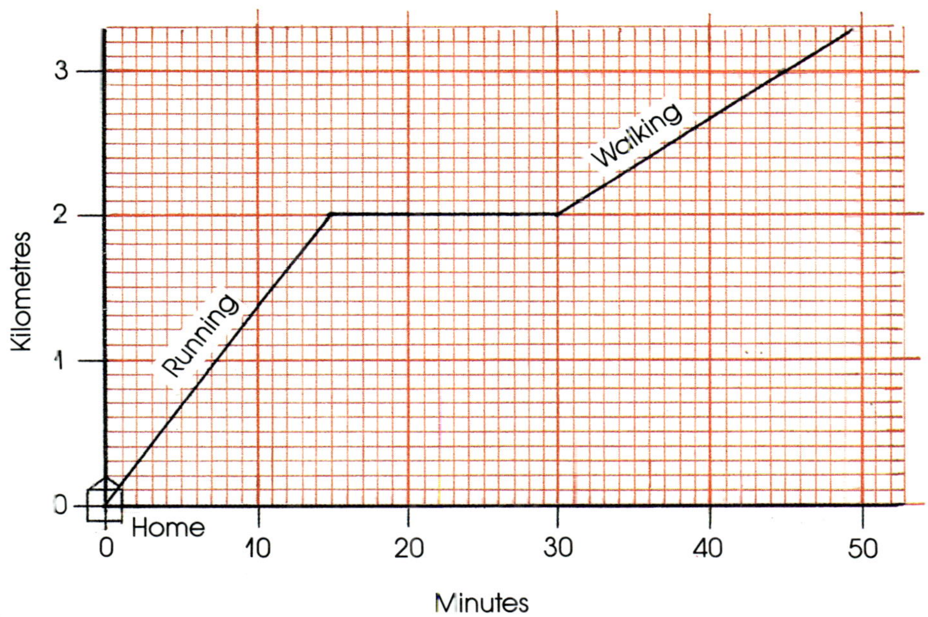

How far from home was Mary after:

15 min? ______ km

20 min? ______ km

30 min? ______ km

After how many minutes was she

3 km from home? ______ 1 km from home? ______

Chance

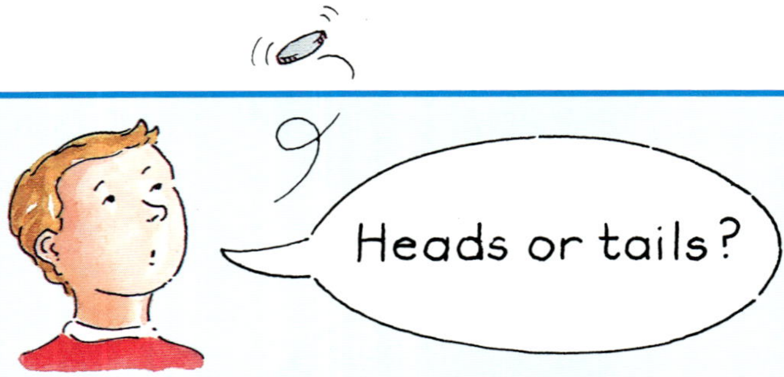

A **fair** coin has **equal** chances of falling **head** or **tail**.

After tossing a coin 100 times Ian got these heads (H) and tails (T).

Tally his results in the table.

THTHHHTTHTTHTTHHTHTHTHHHTHTH

HTHTHHTHTTHTHHTTHHTTHTHT

HHTHTHTTHHTTHTHTTHTTHHT

THHTTHTTHTHHTHTHTHTHTHHTHH

Ian's first tally

	Heads	Tails
Total		

Do you think this is a fair coin? Yes ☐ No ☐

Tally these heads and tails after a different coin was tossed 100 times.

THTHHTHTHTHTHHTTHTHT

HHTHTHHTHTHHTHTHHTTH

THHTHTHHTHHTTHHTTHHH

HHTHHTHHHTHTHHTHHTHH

HTTHHHTHTHHTHHTHTHHT

Ian's second tally

	Heads	Tails
Total		

Do you think this a fair coin? Yes ☐ No ☐

If a fair coin is tossed 200 times:

how many times should it fall **heads**? ☐

how many times should it fall **tails**? ☐

If a fair coin is tossed 2000 times:

how many times should it fall **heads**? ☐

how may times should it fall **tails**? ☐

This is a fair dice numbered

1, 2, 3, 4, 5, 6.

The dice was rolled 120 times.

Finish the totals in this table.

Score	1	2	3	4	5	6
Tally	𝍸 𝍸 𝍸 𝍸 |	𝍸 𝍸 𝍸 ||||	𝍸 𝍸 𝍸 𝍸	𝍸 𝍸 𝍸 ||||	𝍸 𝍸 𝍸 𝍸 |	𝍸 𝍸 𝍸 𝍸
Total number of times scored	21					

Another dice numbered

1, 2, 3, 4, 5, 6

was rolled 120 times.
A graph of the results was drawn.

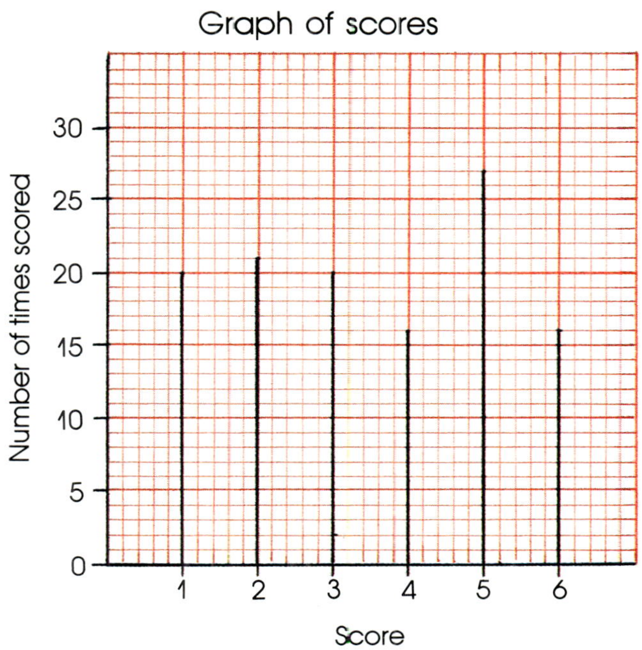

How many times was the score:

1? ☐ 2? ☐

3? ☐ 4? ☐

5? ☐ 6? ☐

Is this a fair dice? Yes ☐ No ☐

Tenths and hundredths

Write these fractions as decimals.

$\frac{1}{10}$ = 0. ____	$\frac{2}{10}$ = 0. ____	$\frac{3}{10}$ = ____
$\frac{4}{10}$ = ____	$\frac{5}{10}$ = ____	$\frac{6}{10}$ = ____
$\frac{7}{10}$ = ____	$\frac{8}{10}$ = ____	$\frac{9}{10}$ = ____
$\frac{1}{100}$ = 0.0 ____	$\frac{7}{100}$ = ____	$\frac{3}{100}$ = ____
$\frac{9}{100}$ = ____	$\frac{2}{100}$ = ____	$\frac{8}{100}$ = ____

Write down the decimal shown by each arrow on this number line.

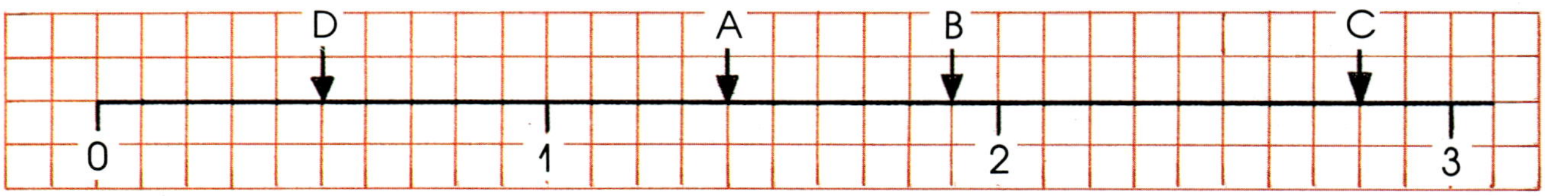

A is 1. ____ B is ____ C is ____ D is ____

On the number line below mark:

A↓ 0.3 ✓	B↓ 0.7	C↓ 0.6
D↓ 0.03	E↓ 0.07	F↓ 0.16

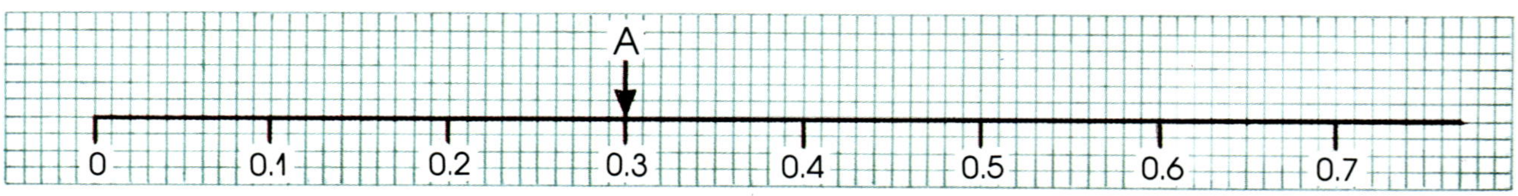

On the number line below mark:

P↓ 0.25	Q↓ 0.75	R↓ C.35
X↓ 0.62	Y↓ 0.69	Z↓ C.48

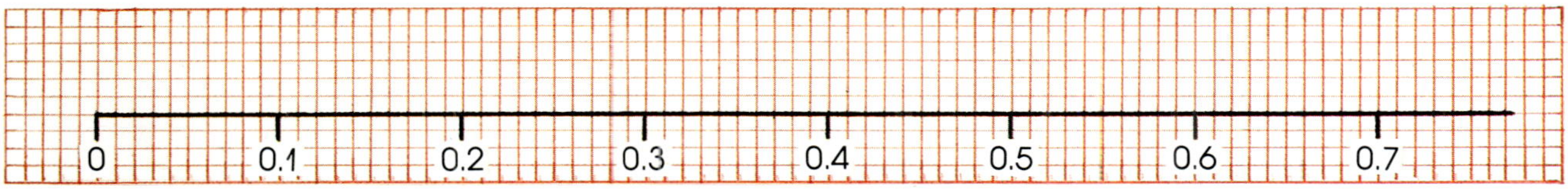

Use the number lines to help you answer these questions.

Which decimal is halfway between 1 and 2? [1.]

Which decimal is halfway between 1.4 and 1.6? [ ]

Which decimal is halfway between 1.3 and 1.9? [ ]

Do these additions and subtractions.

0.2 +0.9 ____	0.3 +0.8 ____	£0.40 +£0.70 £____	£0.50 +£0.60 £____
1.25 +0.25 ____	1.35 +0.15 ____	£0.54 +£0.67 £____	£1.33 +£1.48 £____
0.9 −0.4 ____	1.4 −0.9 ____	£1.30 −£0.80 £____	£1.40 −£0.90 £____
2.25 −1.06 ____	2.25 −0.06 ____	£2.25 −£1.16 £____	£2.25 −£0.26 £____

Which is greater 0.2 or 0.07? [ ]

Which is greater 0.25 or 0.3? [ ]

Is 0.6 greater than, less than or equal to ⅗? [ ]

Fractions

Put the missing fractions in these sentences.

Tammy and Tom together will have $\square$ of the cake.

Tammy, Mary and Ian together will have $\square$ of the cake.

When Tom takes his piece first there will be $\square$ left.

Colour ½ of this square. Colour ¼ of this one. Colour ¾ of this one.

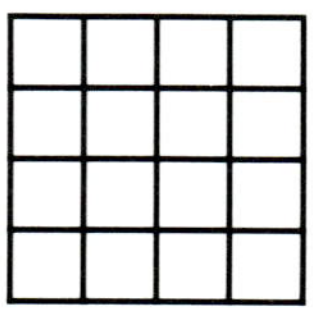

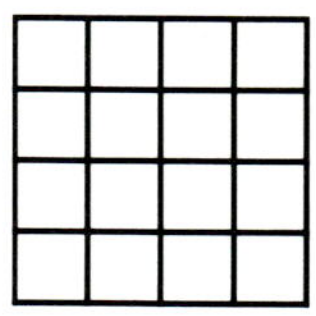

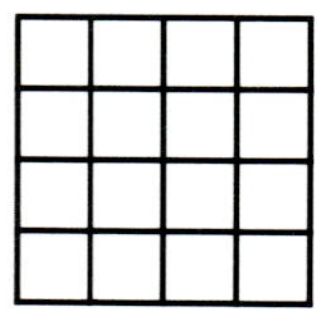

Write the missing fractions on these charts.

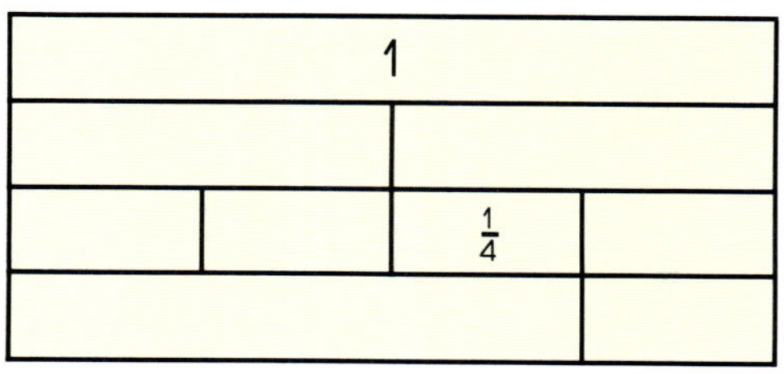

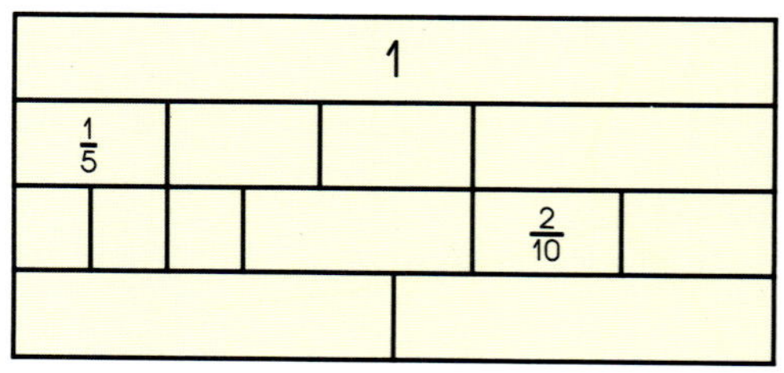

Use the charts to help you fill in these boxes.

$\frac{1}{2} = \frac{\square}{10}$ $\frac{4}{10} = \frac{\square}{5}$ $\frac{2}{4} = \frac{\square}{2}$

$\frac{3}{5} = \frac{\square}{10}$ $\frac{8}{10} = \frac{\square}{5}$ $\frac{2}{10} = \frac{\square}{5}$

$1 = \frac{\square}{4}$ $1 = \frac{\square}{10}$ $1 = \frac{\square}{5}$

Do these additions.

$\frac{1}{4} + \frac{1}{2} =$ $\frac{3}{4} + \frac{1}{4} =$ $\frac{3}{4} + \frac{3}{4} =$

$\frac{1}{5} + \frac{3}{5} =$ $\frac{2}{5} + \frac{3}{5} =$ $\frac{3}{5} + \frac{3}{5} =$

$\frac{3}{10} + \frac{3}{10} =$ $\frac{3}{10} + \frac{7}{10} =$ $\frac{3}{10} + \frac{3}{10} =$

Do these subtractions.

$\frac{3}{4} - \frac{1}{2} =$ $\frac{7}{10} - \frac{4}{10} =$ $\frac{3}{5} - \frac{2}{5} =$

$1 - \frac{1}{4} =$ $1 - \frac{3}{5} =$ $1\frac{3}{5} - \frac{1}{5} =$

$1\frac{1}{2} - \frac{3}{4} =$ $1\frac{1}{4} - \frac{3}{4} =$ $1\frac{2}{5} - \frac{4}{5} =$

Eighths

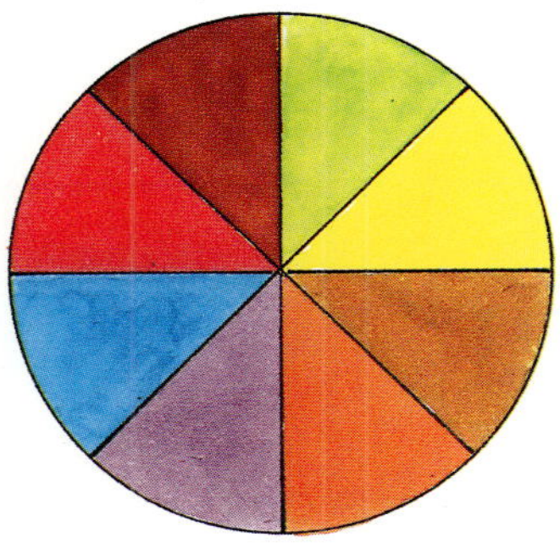

Change these fractions to ⅛ths.

$\frac{1}{2} = \frac{\square}{8}$ $\frac{1}{4} = \frac{\square}{8}$ $\frac{3}{4} = \frac{\square}{8}$

Is $\frac{5}{8}$ greater than $\frac{1}{2}$? ________

Is $\frac{5}{8}$ less than $\frac{3}{4}$? ________

Fill in the missing numbers.

$\frac{1}{2} = \frac{\square}{4} = \frac{\square}{8}$ $\frac{1}{2} = \frac{\square}{4} = \frac{\square}{10}$ $\frac{4}{4} = \frac{\square}{8} = \frac{\square}{10}$

Work these out.

$\frac{3}{5} + \frac{3}{10} = \frac{\square}{10}$ $\frac{2}{5} + \frac{1}{2} = \frac{\square}{10}$ $\frac{1}{5} + \frac{7}{10} = \frac{\square}{10}$

$\frac{1}{2} + \frac{3}{8} = \frac{\square}{8}$ $\frac{1}{4} + \frac{3}{8} = \frac{\square}{8}$ $\frac{1}{8} + \frac{3}{4} = \frac{\square}{8}$

Use $<$ for **less than,** $>$ for **more than** and $=$ for **equal to**.

$\frac{1}{4} < \frac{1}{2}$ $\frac{3}{4} > \frac{1}{4}$ $\frac{2}{4} = \frac{1}{2}$

Put $<$, $>$ or $=$ in each box to make these correct.

$\frac{1}{2} \square \frac{5}{10}$ $\frac{1}{2} \square \frac{2}{5}$ $\frac{1}{2} \square \frac{3}{5}$

$\frac{1}{4} \square \frac{3}{10}$ $\frac{1}{4} \square \frac{2}{10}$ $\frac{2}{4} \square \frac{1}{2}$

$\frac{4}{10} \square \frac{2}{5}$ $\frac{5}{10} \square \frac{3}{4}$ $\frac{5}{10} \square \frac{4}{5}$

Grids and scales

Measure the length of Fred. ______ cm

Measure the length of Fred's friend. ______ cm

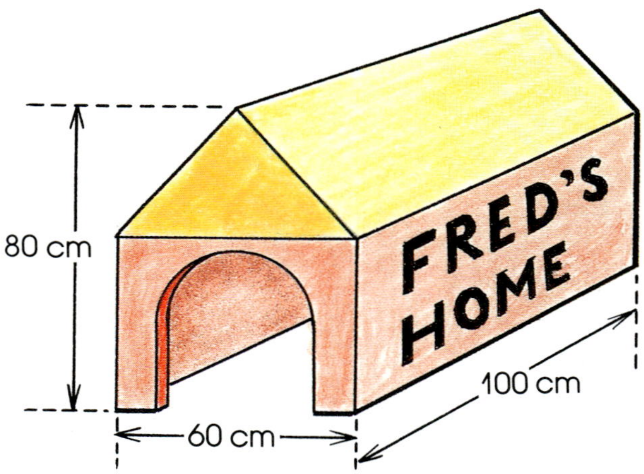

Fred's friend needs a kennel which is ½ as long as Fred's.

Fill in the measurements for the new kennel.
Keep it the same shape as Fred's.

Length ______ cm

Width ______ cm

Height ______ cm

Write down the pair of coordinates for each corner of Fred's garden.

A is (1 , __)　B is (7 , __)

C is (__ , __)　D is (__ , __)

E is (__ , __)　F is (__ , __)

With a scale 1cm represents 1m:

the scale length of AB is ____ cm,

the real length of AB is ____ m.

Scale: 1cm represents 1m

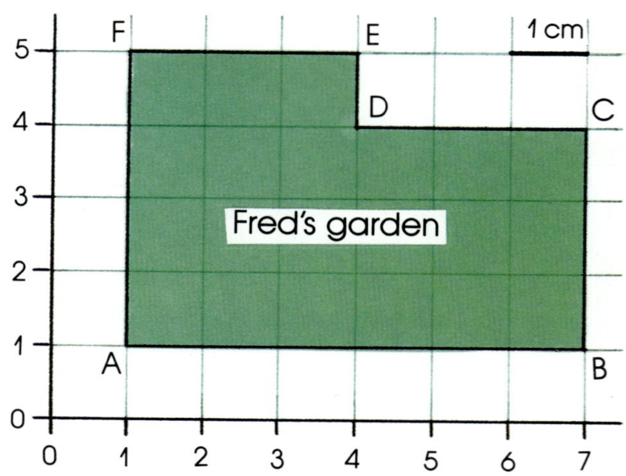

the scale length of BC is ____ cm, the real length is ____ m.

the scale length of AF is ____ cm, the real length is ____ m.

the scale length of FE is ____ cm, the real length is ____ m.

the scale length of ED is ____ cm, the real length is ____ m.

On the scale drawing of Fred's garden (ABCDEF)
the perimeter is ____ cm,
the real perimeter is ____ metres.

On the scale drawing the area is ____ square cm,
the real area is ____ square metres.

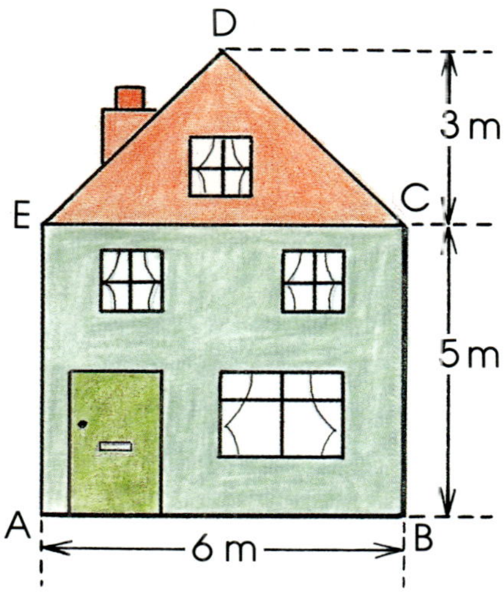

This is a sketch of the house of Fred's owner.

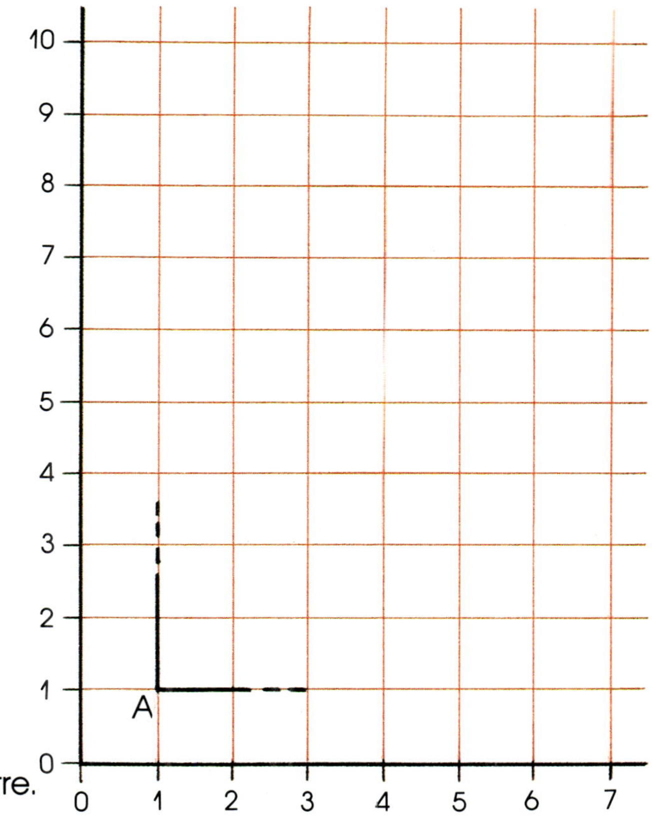

Draw a plan of the house.

Use a scale: 1cm represents 1 metre.

A is the point (1,1) on your plan.
Which pair of coordinates represents:

B? (__, __)   C? (__, __)   D? (__, __)

Count squares and parts of squares to find the area of the front of the house.

Scale area = ______ square cm

Real area = ______ square m

Adding and subtracting

The tortoise is
102 years old.

Ian is
9 years old.

102 + 9 = 111 The ages add up to 111 years.

102 − 9 = 93 The difference in ages is 93 years.

Adding and subtracting will help you to answer these.

15 years ago the tortoise was ______ years old.

In 15 years time Ian will be ______ years old.

Finish these addition trains.

27 + 27 54	54 + 27 ___	+ 27 ___	+ 27 ___	+ 27 ___
103 +103 ___	+ 103 ___	+ 103 ___	+ 103 ___	+ 103 ___
233 + 233 ___	+ 233 ___	+ 233 ___	+ 233 ___	+ 233 ___
209 + 209 ___	+ 209 ___	+ 209 ___	+ 209 ___	+ 209 ___

Fill in these addition squares. Add ⟷ Add ↕

26	27	28	81
25	27	29	
24	27	30	
			243

43	42	41	
44	44	44	
45	46	47	

55	54	53	
54	55	53	
53	54	55	

Finish these subtraction trains.

999 − 222 = 777 → 777 − 222 = ___ → ___ − 222 = ___ → ___ − 222 = ___

902 − 106 = ___ → ___ − 106 = ___ → ___ − 106 = ___ → ___ − 106 = ___

795 − 131 = ___ → ___ − 131 = ___ → ___ − 131 = ___ → ___ − 131 = ___

896 − 224 = ___ → ___ − 224 = ___ → ___ − 224 = ___ → ___ − 224 = ___

Work out these addition and subtraction sums.

1573 + 297 = ___ 1357 + 297 = ___ 1375 + 297 = ___ 1735 + 297 = ___

1573 − 297 = ___ 1357 − 297 = ___ 1375 − 297 = ___ 1735 − 297 = ___

Length

This line is 1 cm long.

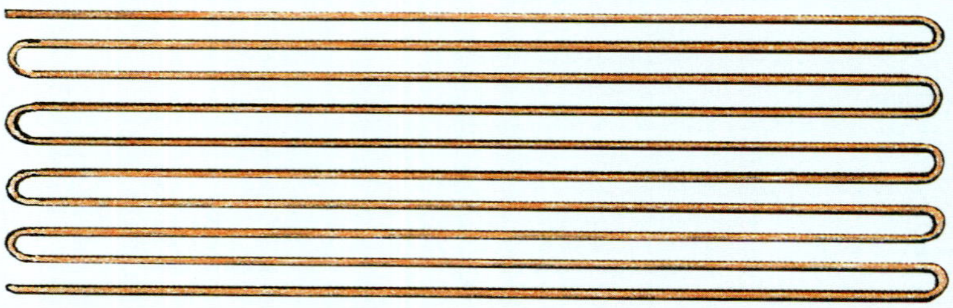

This piece of string is about 1 metre long.

100 cm = 1 metre

1000 metres = 1 kilometre

Ian cut 17 cm of string from a 1 metre length.

What length did Ian leave? ______ cm

Mary cut 25 cm from the piece left.

What length did Mary leave? ______ cm

May has to run 1 kilometre.

After 1 minute she has run 190 metres.

How much further has she to run? ______ metres

In the second minute May runs 210 metres.

May still has to run ______ metres.

Change these lengths to centimetres.

1 m 50 cm = ______ cm

1 m 5 cm = ______ cm

$\frac{1}{4}$ metre = ______ cm

$\frac{1}{10}$ metre = ______ cm

Change these lengths to metres.

1 km 500 m = ______ m

1 km 50 m = ______ m

1 km 5 m = ______ m

$\frac{1}{2}$ kilometre = ______ m

$2\frac{1}{2}$ km = ______ m

$\frac{1}{10}$ kilometre= ______ m

$\frac{1}{100}$ km = ______ m

$\frac{1}{1000}$ km = ______ m

Work out the answers to these sums.

m	cm		m	cm		m	cm		
2	75		5	30		1	30		1 metre ÷ 5
+1	75		−2	55			×4		= ______ cm
______			______			______			

km	m		km	m		km	m		
2	600		3	400		1	500		1 km ÷ 5
+1	500		−1	600			×4		= ______ m
______			______			______			

km	m		km	m		km	m		
3	750		4	260		2	250		2 km ÷ 4
+1	340		−1	360			×4		= ______ m
______			______			______			

This graph shows the distance travelled by a cyclist.

Use the graph to help you work out the distance travelled in:

10 minutes ______ km,

20 minutes ______ km,

30 minutes ______ km,

15 minutes ______ km,

25 minutes ______ km.

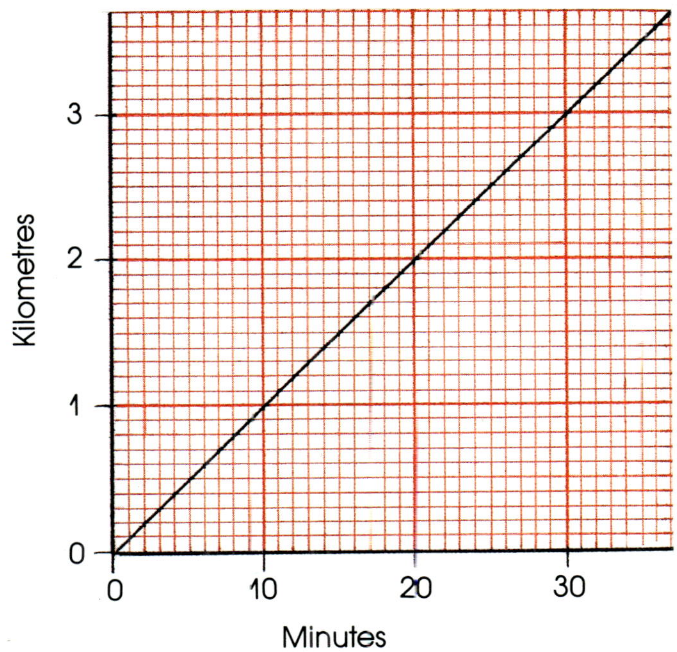

My car is either 400 cm long or 40 m long.

Which length is it? ______

How many centimetres make 1 kilometre? ______

Percentages

10% is read as **ten per cent**.

10% means **10** per **100** which is $\frac{10}{100} = \frac{1}{10}$ or 0.1.

Fill in the fractions and decimals for these percentages.

Percentage	Fraction	Decimal
10%	$\frac{10}{100} = \frac{\square}{10}$	0.1
20%	$\frac{20}{100} = \frac{\square}{10}$	0.2
30%		
40%		
50%		
60%		
70%		
80%		
90%		

A **cent**urion was a Roman soldier.

He had **100** men under his command.

For the centurion:

50 of his 100 men will be ______ % or $\frac{50}{100} = \frac{1}{2}$,

25 of his 100 men will be ______ % or $\frac{\square}{100} = \frac{\square}{4}$,

75 of his 100 men will be ______ % or $\square = \square$.

From the centurion's 100 soldiers how many will be:

10% ? $\square$ 15% ? $\square$ 60% ? $\square$

Work out these percentages for an army of 200 soldiers.

$50\% \text{ of } 200 = \frac{50}{100} \text{ of } 200$

$= \frac{1}{2} \text{ of } 200$

$=$

$25\% \text{ of } 200 =$

$=$

$=$

75% of 200

$=$

10% of 200

$=$

A grocer finds that 10% of his tomatoes are bad.

How many will be bad in:

a box of 100? $\square$ a box of 200? $\square$

a box of 1000? $\square$ a box of 2000? $\square$

Colour 50% of each rectangle in red,
25% in blue, 10% in green
and 5% in black.

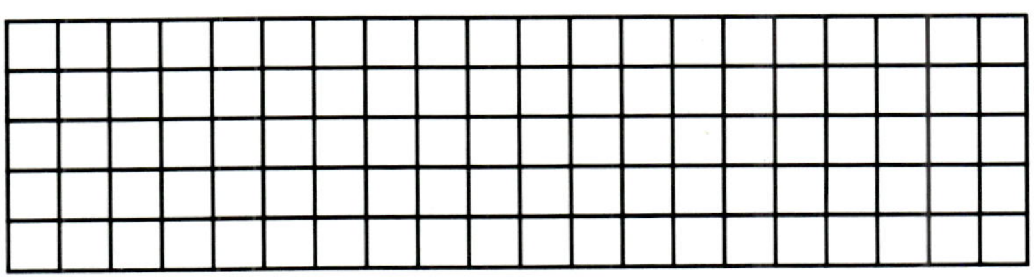

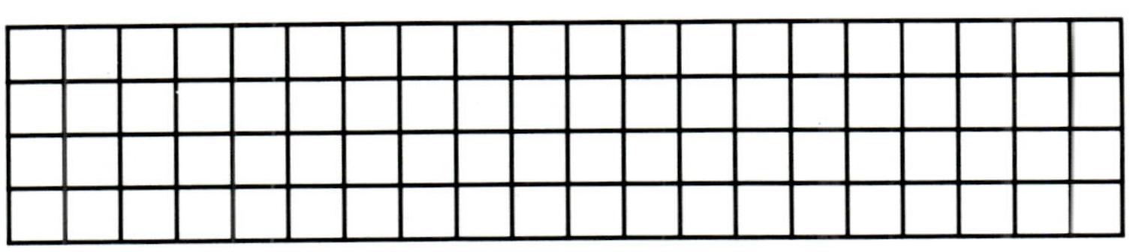

Weight

This is a graph of the weights of Ann, Tom and Emma.

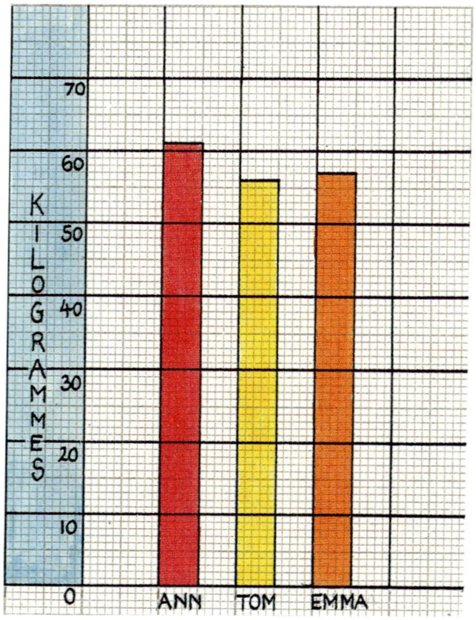

Fill in this table.

Ann ________ kg

Tom ________ kg

Emma ________ kg

Total ________ kg

Divide the weight by 3 to find the average weight of the 3 children.

________kg

By how much is Ann heavier than Emma? ________ kg

By how much is Tom lighter than Ann? ________ kg

Write down the answers.

500g × 4 = ________ kg

500g × 10 = ________ kg

2kg 500g × 2 = ________ kg

2kg 250g × 4 = ________ kg

250g ÷ 5 = ________ g

1kg 250g ÷ 5 = ________ g

1½kg ÷ 3 = ________ g

2½kg ÷ 5 = ________ g

This is a graph of the weight of litter collected on a sponsored 'clean-up'.

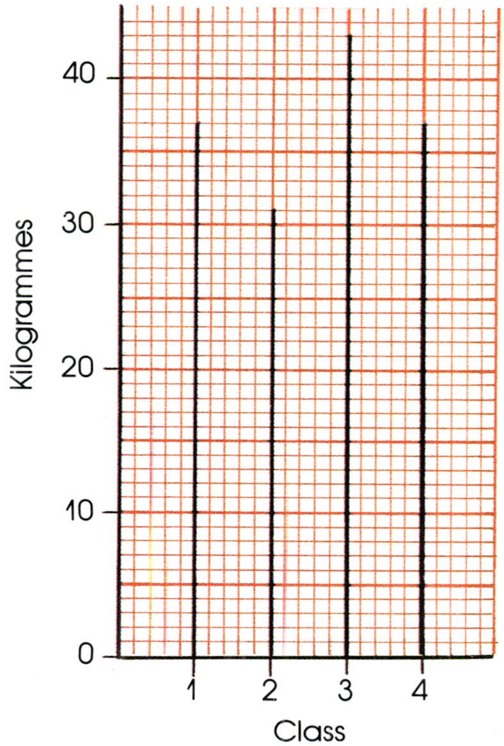

What weight was collected by:

Class 1? ______ kg

Class 2? ______ kg

Class 3? ______ kg

Class 4? ______ kg

The total collected was ______ kg.

What was the average weight collected?

______ kg

At £2.50 per kg collected how much was raised from sponsors by:

Class 1? £ ______ Class 2? £ ______

Class 3? £ ______ Class 4? £ ______

This graph shows the weight of sweets sold in the school tuck-shop.

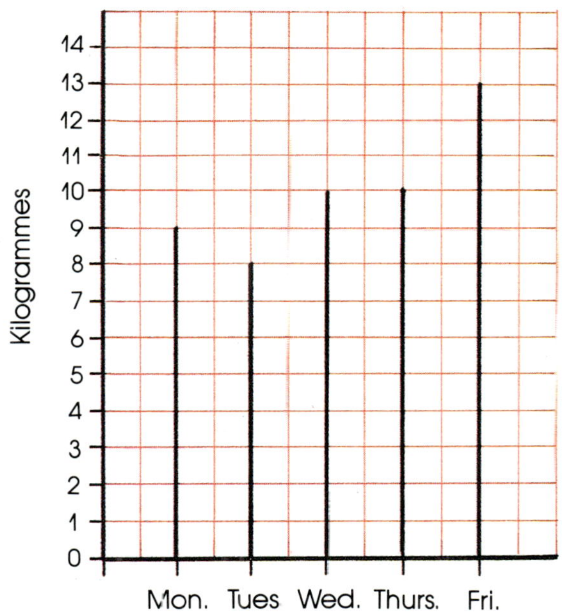

Which day had the:

highest sale? ______

lowest sale? ______

What was the total sale for the week?

kg

kg

kg

kg

______ kg

Total ______ kg

What was the average daily weight sold? ______ kg

At £4.50 per kg what were the takings on Monday? £ ______

Area and volume

Write down the number of square centimetres covered by each shape.

Shape	Square cm
1	
2	
3	
4	
5	
6	
7	

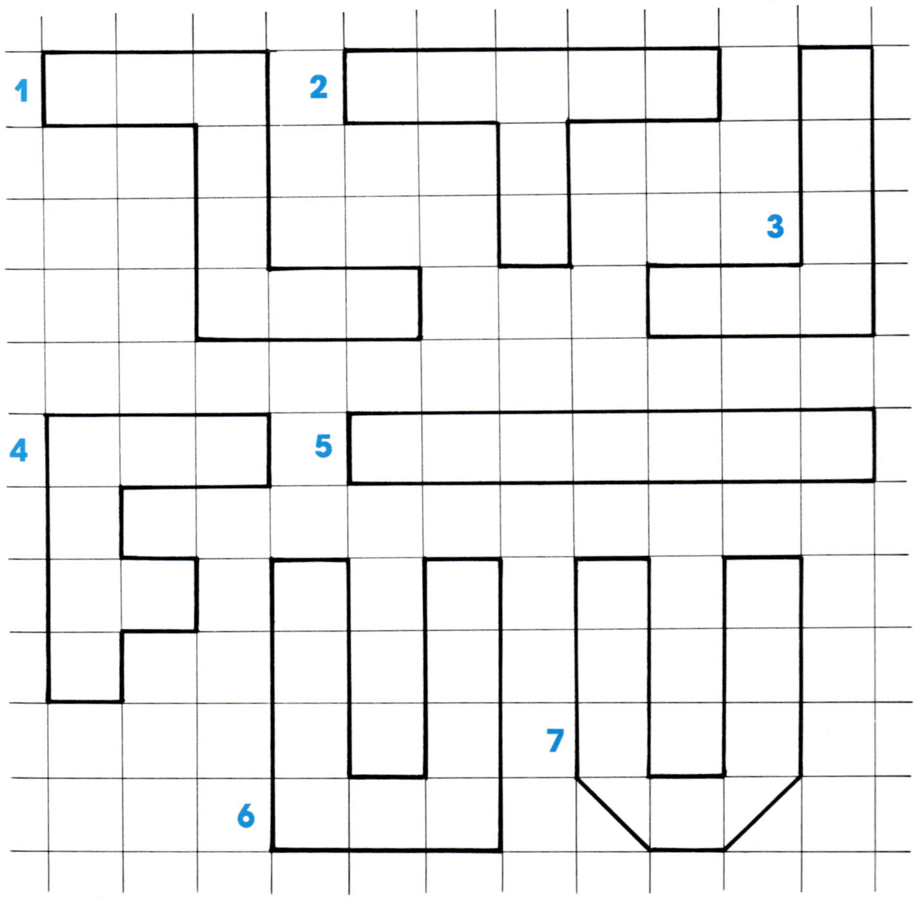

Which one of the shapes covers the most area? Number ______

Which one of the shapes covers the least area? Number ______

Which shapes have an area of:

7 square cm? ______ , ______ , ______ 8 square cm? ______ , ______

On this grid of cm squares draw:

1 a square with area **16** square cm.

2 a square with area **9** square cm.

3 a rectangle **3** squares wide with an area of **15** square cm.

4 a rectangle with area **21** square cm.

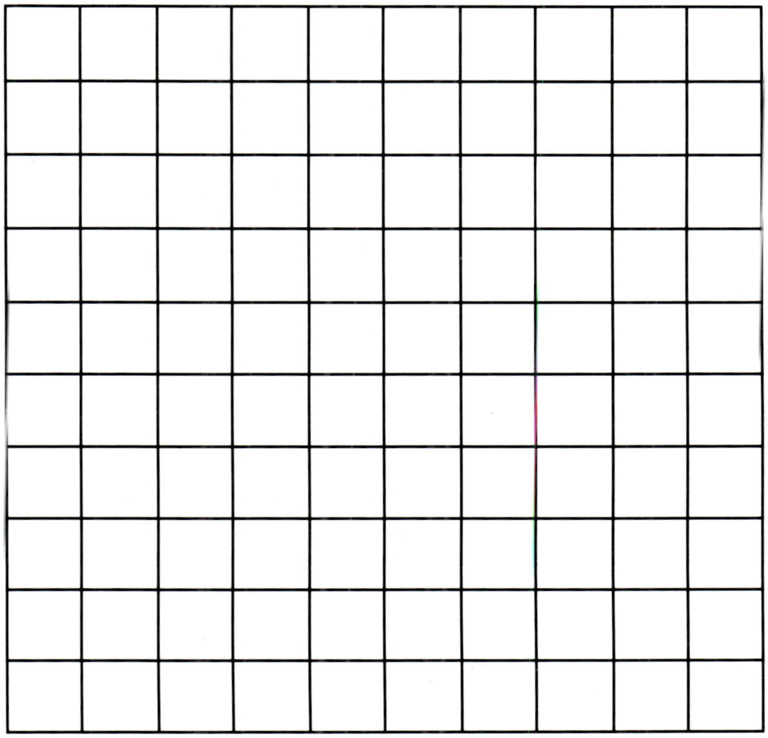

The space in this box is to be filled with 1 cm cubes.

How many cubes will fit on the bottom?

________ cubes

How many cubes will fill the box?

________ cubes

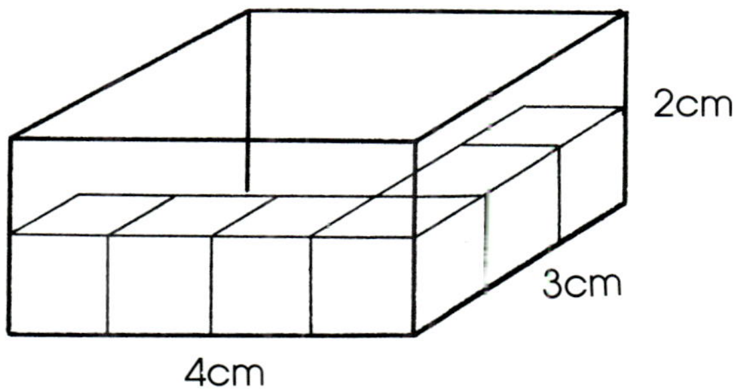

How many 1 cm cubes will fill each of these boxes?

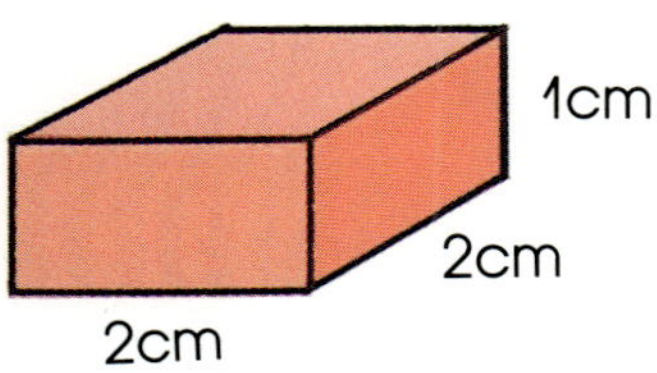

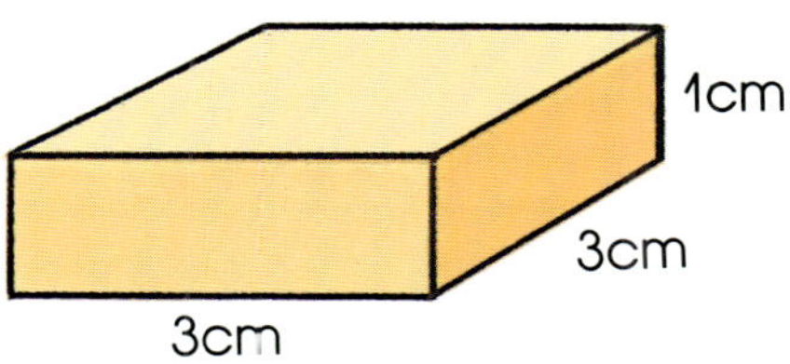

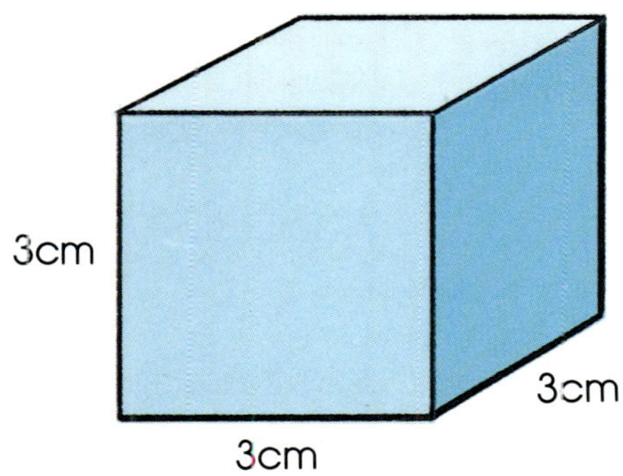

________ cubes

________ cubes

________ cubes

Shapes and angles

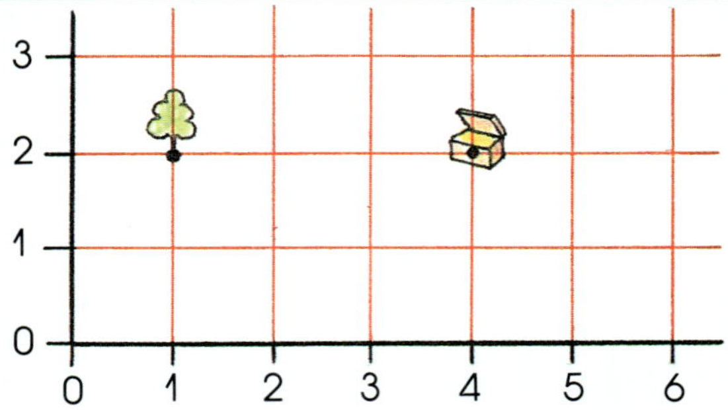

The tree is at the point with coordinates (1,2).

You must dig for treasure at point (4,2).

Join point **B** to point (1,7).

Join point **A** to point (1,7).

What shape have you drawn?

____

What is the name of the angle you have made at **B**?

____

How many degrees is the angle at **B**?

____

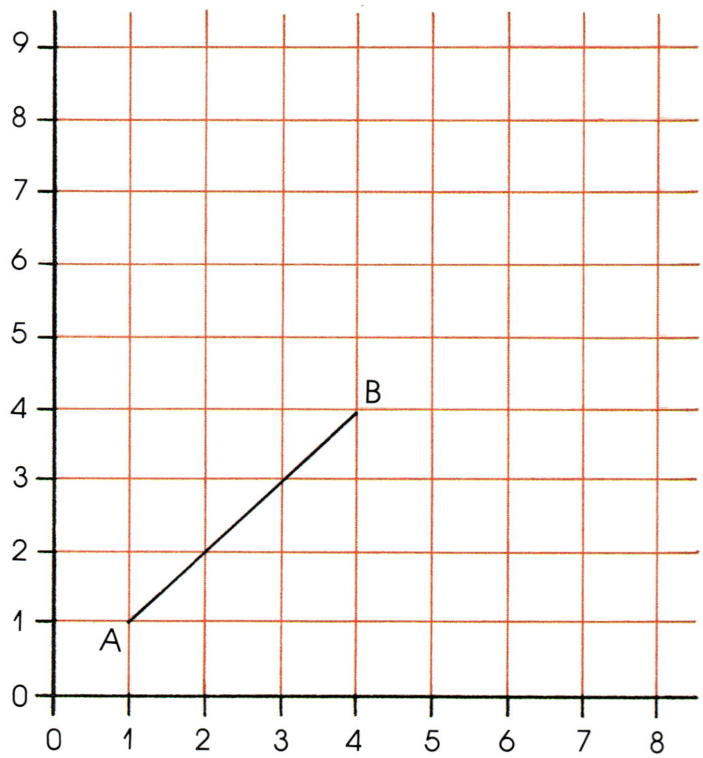

Now start at (4,0) and draw a line parallel to line **AB** and the same length as **AB**.

Where does your line finish? (____ , ____)

Join these points in order:

(3,6) ⟶ (7,6) ⟶ (8,8) ⟶ (4,8) ⟶ (3,6).

What is the name of the shape you have drawn? ________

Which one of these angles is called:

acute? Number ______

obtuse? Number ______

reflex? Number ______

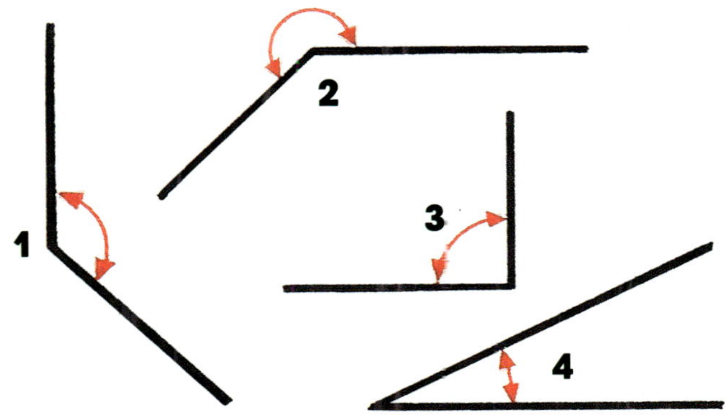

Draw these shapes full size and as accurately as you can.

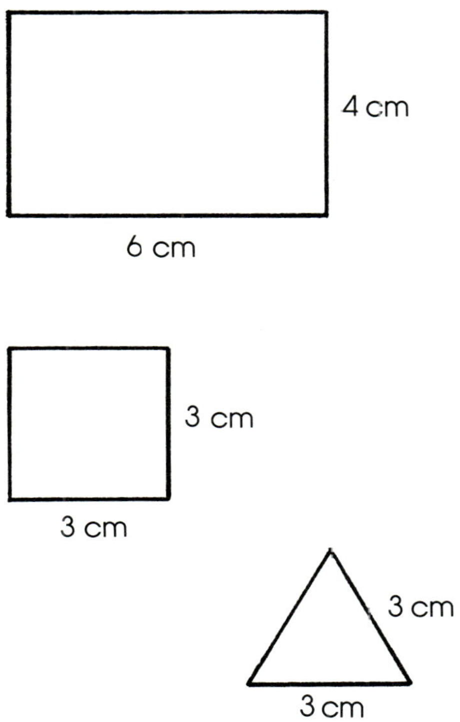

This line | is a line of symmetry for each road sign.

Finish drawing the road signs.

Calculation

Ian did this division.

$\frac{1}{5} = 1 \div 5 = 0.2$

Mary tried this one but couldn't seem to finish it.

$\frac{1}{3} = 1 \div 3 = 0.333333$

Check Ian's sum on a calculator.

$1 \div 5 =$ ______

Check Mary's sum on a calculator.

$1 \div 3 =$ ______

Mary's aunt had her lunch and counted the calories.

Total the calories for Mary's aunt.

Calorie count	Calories
1 boiled egg	85
2 slices of bread	135
butter	54
2 cups of coffee	65
1 small cake	77
Total	

Change these fractions to decimals.

$\frac{1}{2} =$ $\frac{1}{4} =$ $\frac{3}{4} =$

$\frac{1}{10} =$ $\frac{7}{10} =$ $\frac{3}{10} =$

$\frac{1}{5} =$ $\frac{2}{5} =$ $\frac{3}{5} =$

Do these sums without a calculator and then check your answer with a calculator.

$424 \div 8 =$ ______ $420 \div 8 =$ ______ $480 \div 80 =$ ______

$631 \times 5 =$ ______ $632 \times 5 =$ ______ $633 \times 5 =$ ______

$723 \div 3 =$ ______ $723 \div 30 =$ ______ $72.3 \div 3 =$ ______

$420 \times 6 =$ ______ $42 \times 60 =$ ______ $420 \times 60 =$ ______

$75 \times 4 \div 3 =$ ______ $56 \times 9 \div 7 =$ ______

$9 \times 9 \times 9 =$ ______ $11 \times 11 \times 11 =$ ______

Check these patterns and write the next two lines of each one.
Check by using a calculator.

$1 \times 9 + 2 =$ 11	$37037 \times 6 =$ 222222
$12 \times 9 + 3 =$ 111	$37037 \times 9 =$ 333333
$123 \times 9 + 4 =$ ☐	$37037 \times 12 =$ ☐
☐ $\times 9 +$ ☐ $=$ ☐	☐ $\times$ ☐ $=$ ☐

$1 \times 1 =$ 1	$33 \times 37 =$ 1221
$11 \times 11 =$ 121	$333 \times 37 =$ 12321
$111 \times 111 =$ ☐	☐ $\times 37 =$ ☐
☐ $\times$ ☐ $=$ ☐	☐ $\times$ ☐ $=$ ☐

Answer these puzzles. Use a calculator if you need to.

Ian thinks of a number, doubles it, adds 5 and gets the answer 25. What was Ian's number? ☐

Mary thinks of a number, halves it, adds 5 and gets the answer 10. What was her number? ☐

Which number multiplied by itself and then by 2 becomes 98? ☐

Which is the lowest number divisible by 3, 5 and 7? ☐

Which is the lowest number divisible by 4, 8 and 9? ☐

Answers

To Parents: We have not provided *all* the answers here. We suggest that items to be drawn should be checked by you. In the case of activities where calculations are performed by your child, it would be good practice to get him/her to use a calculator to check the answers.

Page 2

8 4 2
8 4

31 63

1110 1000 1000 1030

202 98 363 198

Page 3

193 411 380 701 600

201 199 209 241 251

301 122 245 44
99 278 155 356

6 4 5 5
5 7 7 6

7 6 6 7
4 4 7 6

Page 4

3000 4500 6000 7500

3000
3000 6000
4500 9000
6000

7500 9000 10500 12000
375 378 738 1110

Page 5

1845 1424 2100 1791

×	1	2	3	4	5	6	7	8	9	10
1	1	2	3	4	5	6	7	8	9	10
2	2	4	6	8	10	12	14	16	18	20
3	3	6	9	12	15	18	21	24	27	30
4	4	8	12	16	20	24	28	32	36	40
5	5	10	15	20	25	30	35	40	45	50
6	6	12	18	24	30	36	42	48	54	60
7	7	14	21	28	35	42	49	56	63	70
8	8	16	24	32	40	48	56	64	72	80
9	9	18	27	36	45	54	63	72	81	90
10	10	20	30	40	50	60	70	80	90	100

860 2160 1827 747
1836 1476 4527 2919

Page 6

24 48 12 6 4 40

21 28 14 12
210 168 140 120
420 260 105 84
402 268 134 68

Page 7

25 12,2 8,2
250,0 125,0 83,2
5,0 6,2 16,2
50,0 62,4 166,2

Page 7 (cont)

9
5
2,4,7
2,3,4,6,8,12
2,3,4,6,9,12,18
1,29

55 45,5 39,2
51,3 126,2 112,4
106,4 99 101,1

Page 8

8 12
10 6
20 60 2

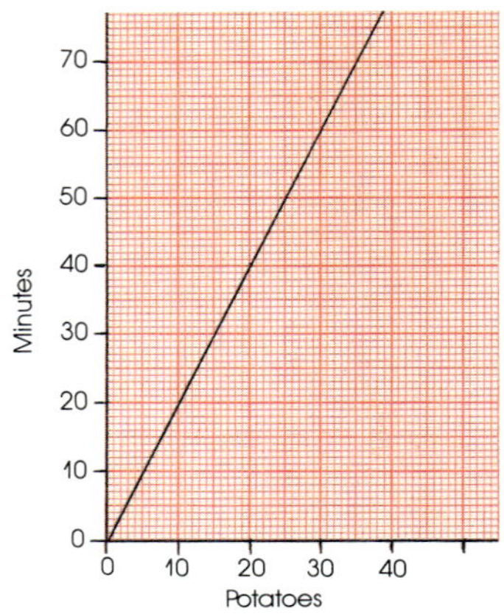

Page 9

10 20 10
30 5 5

2 2 2
45 7½

Page 10

First tally : heads : 51,
tails : 49
Yes
Second tally : heads : 60,
tails : 40
No

Page 11

100 100 1000 1000

Score: 2 3 4 5 6
Total 19 20 19 21 20

20 21
20 16
27 16
No

Page 12

0.1 0.2 0.3
0.4 0.5 0.6
0.7 0.8 0.9
0.01 0.07 0.03
0.09 0.02 0.08

1.4 1.9 2.8 0.5

Page 12 (cont)

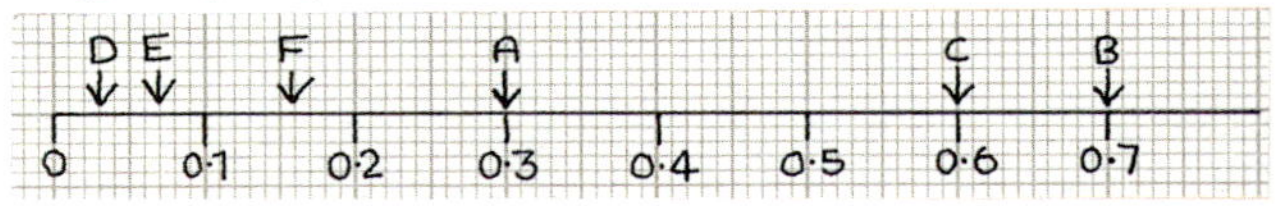

Page 13

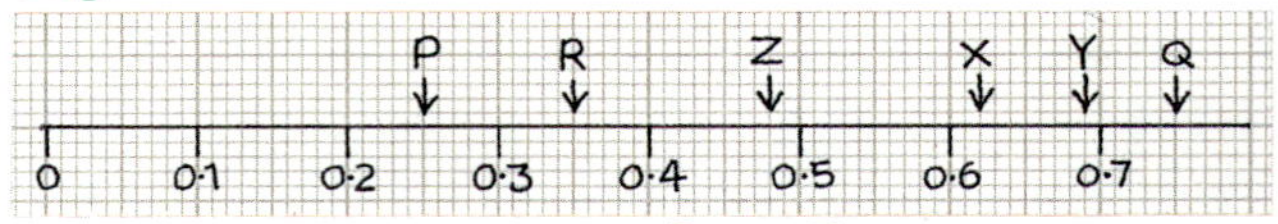

1.5 1.5 1.6

1.1 1.1 1.10 1.10
1.5 1.5 1.21 2.81
0.5 0.5 0.50 0.50
1.19 2.19 1.09 1.99

0.2 0.3 equal to

Page 14

½ ¾ ¾

Colour ½ = 8 squares
Colour ¼ = 4 squares
Colour ¾ = 12 squares

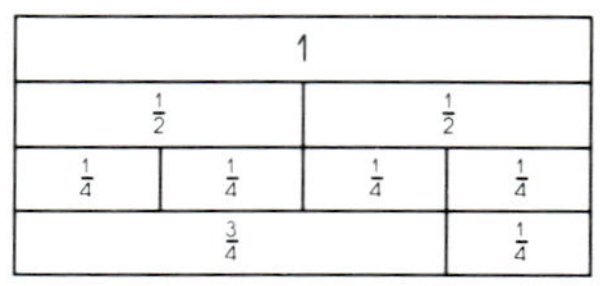

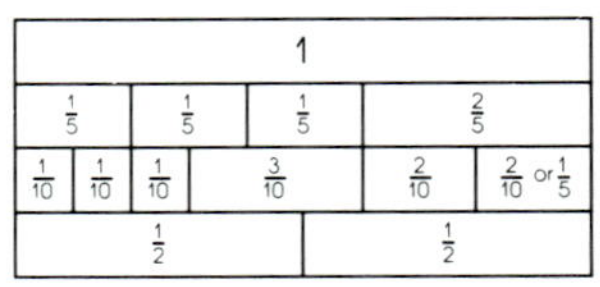

5 2 1
6 4 1
4 10 5

Page 15

¾ 1 1½
⅘ 1 1⅕
⅗ 1 1⅒

¼ 3/10 ⅕
¾ ⅖ 1⅖
¾ ½ ⅗

4 2 6
Yes Yes

2,4 2,5 8,10

9 9 9
7 5 7
< > <
< > =
= < <

Page 16

6 3
50 30 40

1 1
7,4 4,4
4,5 1,5

6 6

Page 17

3 3
4 4
3 3
1 1
20 20
21 21

7,1 7,6 4,9
39 39

Page 18

87 24

81 108 135
81 108 135 162

206 309 412 515
206 309 412 515 618

466 699 932 1165
466 699 932 1165 1398

418 627 836 1045
418 627 836 1045 1254

Page 19

81
81
78 81 87

126
132
138
132 132 132 396

162
162
162
162 163 161 486

555 333
555 333 111

796 690 584
796 690 584 478

664 533 402
664 533 402 271

672 448 224
672 448 224 0